"For one human being to love another: that is perhaps the most difficult of all tasks, the ultimate, the last test and proof, the work for which all other work is but preparation ... so we must not forget, when we love, that we are beginners, bunglers of life, apprentices in love and must learn love ..."

~Rainer Maria Rilke

PAIRS Essentials
Practical Skills for Successful Relationships

Printed by CreateSpace, An Amazon.com Company.
Available from Amazon.com and other online stores.

With profound appreciation for the contributions of Virginia Satir, Daniel Casriel, Lori Heyman Gordon, George Bach, Williard Harley, Gary Chapman, John Gray, Seth Eisenberg, and each of those pioneers whose passion for understanding and empowering fulfilling human relationships illuminated our path.

PAIRS Foundation is the sole provider of training, certification and licensure for PAIRS Instructors throughout the world. Our global community of providers deliver PAIRS classes in accordance with rigorous ethical and licensing standards designed to ensure consistent excellence in program delivery and the satisfaction of every program participant. For a list of currently licensed PAIRS Providers and directory of upcoming PAIRS classes, visit consumer.pairs.com.

Published by The PAIRS Foundation, Inc.

The PAIRS Foundation, Inc.
20275 W. Oak Haven Circle
Miami, FL 33179 USA
(877) PAIRS-4U - (877) 724-7748
Email: info@pairs.com
Online at www.pairs.com

Library of Congress Registration: TX0007378687.
ISBN-10: 0985427833.
ISBN-13: 978-0-9854278-3-2.

Manufactured in the United States of America.

PAIRS is a research-validated, highly experiential approach to creating and sustaining successful relationships. Through an innovative, proprietary technology researched and refined over more than a quarter century, PAIRS consistently delivers experiences that empower participants with practical, usable skills to strengthen emotional literacy, empathy, communication, problem-solving, collaboration and - in love relationships - bonding.

Couples discover greater depths of intimacy.

Knowledge & **practical skills** for enhanced communication, empathy, **emotional** connection, understanding & **love.**

PAIRS
FOUNDATION

Since 1983, the nonprofit PAIRS Foundation's mission has been to help create a safer, saner, more loving world through educational experiences that strengthen human connection, such as the vital interpersonal relationships that are the foundation of successful marriages, partnerships, families, schools, teams, organizations, and workplaces.

PAIRS, which stands for "Practical Application of Intimate Relationship Skills," originally emerged out of a multi-decade search for answers to all the questions of what it took not to fall in love — that's the easy part — but to sustain healthy, intimate relationships through life's natural passages, transitions, and the challenges that face couples and families across the globe.

The skills delivered in PAIRS classes empower participants with practical, time-tested skills for accurate, authentic communication; deepening empathy and compassion; listening attentively to create an environment of emotional openness and honesty; navigating conflict and differences constructively on behalf of a shared vision and mission; uncovering hidden expectations to avoid assumptions and misunderstandings; recognizing the influence of past experiences; and embracing opportunities for growth, learning and collaboration.

Advanced programs for graduates of PAIRS Essentials include powerful exercises exploring the self and family dynamics; experiencing the depth of human bonding and opportunities for accelerated emotional re-education; expanding sensual and sexual connection; and contracting to negotiate shared power, responsibilities and roles within dynamic peer relationships.

PAIRS programs range from intensive half-day, one-day, weekend workshops and multi-week seminars, to the hallmark 120-hour, semester-long Mastery Course. Classes are facilitated by educators, counselors, health care professionals, clergy and others trained and licensed by the PAIRS Foundation.

PAIRS Foundation's rigorous, multi-level, professional certification training, ethical practices and licensing standards, ongoing research, refinement, and proprietary quality management systems have earned PAIRS the reputation as an industry leader in relationship skills training.

Nine-hour research-validated training delivered over an intensive weekend or consecutive weekly sessions, introduces essential skills for improving communication, self-worth, empathy, emotional expression, and healthy conflict resolution on behalf of lasting breakthroughs in relationship satisfaction.

Thirty-hour evidence-based PAIRS Supporting Healthy Marriages curriculum integrates essential skills training with additional modules on parenting, finance, time management, and social supports; extended classes, instructor and peer coaching support increased retention. Optional case management role.

Weekend and online workshop to explore chemistry, compatibility and commitment. Discover more focused and sensual style of lovemaking, work creatively with differences, deepen intimacy, confiding and bonding, and learn to break-out of cycles of guilt and frustration that can sabotage pleasure.

Ten 60-90 minute age-appropriate classes for youth designed to improve communication, confiding and emotional understanding, increase empathy, compassion, self-esteem, self-worth, constructive conflict resolution, healthy decision-making, forgiveness, and strategies to counter negative peer pressures.

WHAT PEOPLE ARE SAYING

"**Skill-based** love is the most romantic and the most enduring... **PAIRS** is the Cadillac of programs."

Diane Sollee
Founder/ Director
Coalition for Marriage, Family, and Couples Education

Featured in National Media as a Trend Setter for a Quarter Century

PAIRS has been featured and acclaimed in the national media for more than a quarter century, including NBC, ABC, CBS, CNN, MSNBC, CBN, Washington Post, Wall Street Journal, New York Times, TIME, Cosmopolitan, Readers Digest, Good Housekeeping, New Woman, Psychology Today, Atlantic Monthly, Miami Herald, Redbook, Woman's Day, Bill Maher, and many, many more.

"**PAIRS** is **life changing, intense** and **humbling.**"

Michelle Washington, LMSW
US Army

CURRICULUM CONTENTS

INTRODUCTION BY VIRGINIA SATIR

"In a world where equality between human beings is generally not practiced and maybe not known, the material contained in PAIRS is a truly significant, pioneering effort."

As we moved into the 20th century, we arrived with a very clearly prescribed way that males and females in marriage were to behave with one another. The man was the undisputed head of and authority in the family; he was to provide for and protect his wife and children.

The woman's role was to obey her husband, take care of him, take charge of the house, bear and take care of the children and be responsible for setting the emotional tone in the family. She was also responsible for the sexual fidelity of the home. In the marriage vows of the time, women pledged to love, honor and obey; men only had to love and cherish their wives.

Psychologist Virginia Satir (1918-1988), widely considered the "Mother of Family Therapy," significantly influenced the development of PAIRS and served as honorary founding chairperson.

The pattern of the relationship between husband and wife was that of the dominant male and submissive female. Society of that day only gave recognition and status to those who married. Others, who did not marry, especially women, were considered misfits, objects of pity and sometimes scorn. As a result, women scrambled to get married; to be respectable, a woman had to have a Mrs. in her name.

A new era has since dawned. This began when women attained the right to vote in 1920. That gave them control over their lives. Slowly, states began to liberalize divorce laws as well. There had always been divorce possible under the grounds of adultery, insanity and desertion; now, they were being extended to neglect and abuse.

During World War II, much of the work formerly done by men was successfully done by women. This gave women a new sense of confidence. They learned they could be successful heads of families themselves. When the men returned from war, the climate of relationships had changed; women were no longer willing to be submissive.

The women's rights' movement emerged soon thereafter. The end of the dominant/submissive model in relationships was in sight. However, there was very little that had developed to replace the old pattern; couples floundered. New forms for the new values had not yet emerged, and the old ones were no longer acceptable.

The aim was to develop a new kind of equality, based on equal value of each person. Old role definitions were no longer appropriate and chaos was setting in. Retrospectively, one could have expected that there would be a lot of chaos and a lot of fall-out. The change from the dominant/submissive model to one of equality is a monumental shift. We are learning how a relationship based on genuine feelings of equality can operate practically.

PAIRS is a splendid preparation toward enabling couples to develop new satisfying patterns of relationship based on high self-worth for each one. The program of PAIRS touches all the significant variables in the marital relationship. PAIRS emerged out of several hundred seminars with ordinary couples who wanted to reshape their patterns of relationship. PAIRS is the outcome of the experiences of those couples.

CONGRATULATIONS AND WELCOME

"Your faith, courage and commitment is the foundation of our work to help create a safer, saner, more loving world."

Seth and Stephanie Eisenberg

Congratulations, and Welcome to PAIRS!

Your PAIRS experience will introduce you to a treasure chest of tools that have helped tens of thousands around the world create, nurture, restore, and rekindle relationships that are the very foundation of our lives. Since 1983, the nonprofit PAIRS Foundation's dedication to improving the lives of children by helping their parents and other adults who significantly influence their lives build, model, and sustain healthy, loving, joyous relationships has fueled our collective commitment to develop, research, refine and deliver the world's premier relationship skills training programs.

PAIRS Essentials incorporates lessons learned, best practices, and quality management developed out of multi-year research with thousands of diverse men and women in all stages of relationship. For the far majority of individuals and couples who arrive at their first PAIRS session open to learning and with goodwill towards each other, PAIRS delivers knowledge and skills that provide significant, enduring benefits. I invite you to learn more about those findings by visiting evaluation.pairs.com.

We are grateful to each of you who participate in PAIRS. Your faith, courage and commitment is an inspiration to all of us dedicated to making PAIRS widely available on behalf of our longstanding vision to help create a safer, saner, more loving world.

We look forward to learning about your personal experience in PAIRS through your end of class evaluation. You can also reach out to us anytime by phone, email or online at www.pairs.com.

Congratulations again on your decision to experience PAIRS. We appreciate the opportunity to share this knowledge with you and trust your highest expectations will be met.

With much appreciation,

Seth D. Eisenberg
President/CEO
The PAIRS Foundation, Inc.

GROUND RULES

1. **Respect each other's privacy.**
   Anything discussed in the PAIRS class is confidential. Confidential means not sharing or discussing any information learned about others in the group with anyone other than your partner.

2. **Sharing with others in the class is voluntary.**
   When doing class activities, you can choose to say and express whatever feelings you have. You can also choose to remain silent. Your silence will be respected.

3. **Speak only for yourself, not your partner.**
   When sharing, make "I" statements rather than "We" statements. For example, say, "I feel" or "I think," but not "We think" or "We feel."

4. **If sharing about your relationship, check it out with your partner first.**
   Checking it out with your partner before sharing something personal about your relationship demonstrates respect, just in case they feel uncomfortable about having the information shared in the class.

5. **A goal of the class is to feel safe, to learn and to have fun.**
   This class experience is unique and is designed so that you experience with your partner a sense of community that is shared with others in the class. This experience of community will help strengthen your relationship.

6. **Be respectful and considerate of others.**
   Turn off your cell phones and other smart devices during class. At times of need it may be necessary that you be reached by phone, text or email. At these times, put your device on vibrate and kindly handle the communication outside the classroom.

7. **Be present.**
   As much as possible, seek to be fully present physically, intellectually, mentally and emotionally to give yourself the greatest opportunity to benefit from your training.

PAIRS
FOUNDATION

THE LANGUAGE OF LOVE

PAIRS has been called the Language of Love. Throughout PAIRS Essentials, you will learn new terms and a unique meaning of some that may already be familiar.

At the heart of PAIRS is a unique technology that combines practical knowledge and skills in an experiential process to empower joyful, fulfilling relationships built on a foundation of goodwill, empathy, and compassion.

- **Goodwill** includes kindness towards others. In PAIRS, goodwill is represented by four c's: commitment, caring, communication and change.

- **Empathy** is the ability to identify with or experience the feelings, thoughts or attitudes of another person.

- **Compassion** is the expression of our desire to alleviate suffering.

- **Bonding** goes beyond the traditional definition of a close relationship that often develops as a result of intense, shared experiences to represent the biologically-based human need for the combination of emotional openness and physical closeness with another person.

Other terms likely to take on new meaning through your PAIRS Essentials training include phrases such as "Relationship Road Map," "Stress Styles," "Leveling," "Daily Temperature Reading," "Empathic Listening," "Talking Tips," "Love Bank," "Emotional Stages," "Emotional Jug," "Time-Out," "Dirty Fighting," "Fair Fight for Change," "Relationship Agreement," "Love Knots," "Powergram," "Emotional Allergies," and "Infinity Loops."

Throughout PAIRS, we encourage you to be a detective on your own behalf, open to exploring, connecting, and growing.

Part of the gift of new experiences such as those offered by PAIRS is that you can try them out -- similar to how you'd try on a new outfit -- and decide what fits for you at a given moment in time and what may not. The goal of PAIRS is to give you the best opportunity for your wishes, hopes and dreams to have the greatest chance of coming true. Embracing the opportunity for learning and discovery will help you decide what will best contribute to the goals and values that are most important to you.

> *"I have sought love, first, because it brings ecstasy - ecstasy so great that I would often have sacrificed all the rest of life for a few hours of this joy. I have sought it, next, because it relieves loneliness - that terrible loneliness in which one shivering consciousness looks over the rim of the world into the cold unfathomable lifeless abyss. I have sought it, finally, because in the union of love I have seen, in a mystic miniature, the prefiguring vision of the heaven that saints and poets have imagined."*
>
> — Bertrand Russell

SESSION ONE

- Relationship Road Map
- Stress Styles of Communication
- Daily Temperature Reading
- Talking Tips
- Love Bank

NOTES:

In addition to the knowledge and skills you will discover in PAIRS Essentials, you can practice and deepen your experience through online adaptations of the exercises at apps.pairs.com. You may also receive important follow-up and supplemental information from PAIRS Foundation to reinforce your workshop experience. You can remind your instructor to email us your class roster promptly to be sure you receive PAIRS Love Notes and other follow-up from PAIRS by email shortly after this class. Please also complete and return the brief survey you will receive. You are important to us!

THE HEART OF INTIMACY

Key Goals

- Learn PAIRS concepts as a framework for understanding the journey of intimacy: Levels of Learning, Stages of Relationship, Three Hopes/Fears, and the Relationship Road Map.

- Identify styles and patterns that influence how we communicate under stress and their impact on close relationships. Learn the Leveling Style that strengthens connection and understanding.

- Learn the Daily Temperature Reading and Talking Tips as tools to enhance and nurture connection, cohesion, empathy and respect between intimates.

- Consider the importance of creating and sustaining pleasure in intimate relationships through the concept of the Love Bank and Caring Behaviors to intentionally nurture a loving environment.

Topics and Tools

- Levels of Learning

- Stages of Relationship

- Three Hopes/Three Fears

- Relationship Road Map

- Stress Styles of Communication

- Leveling Style

- Daily Temperature Reading

- Talking Tips

- Love Bank

- Caring Behaviors

"PAIRS changed a 29-year marriage of confusion, hurt, silence and missed opportunities into a vibrant relationship of pleasure and trust that thrives on change and growth."

WHERE WERE WE SUPPOSED TO HAVE LEARNED?

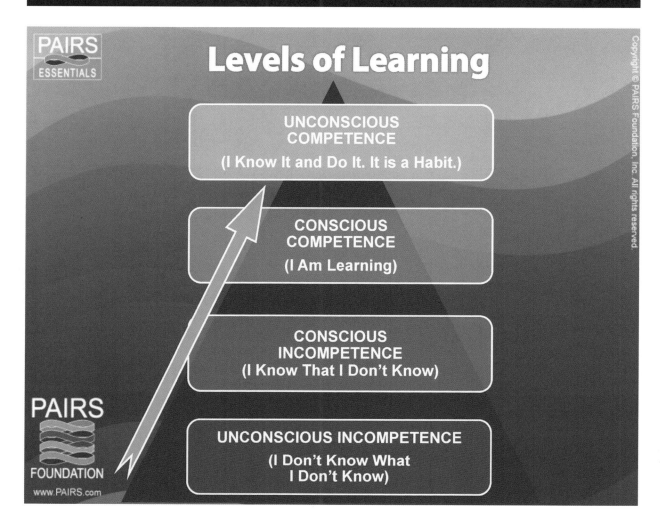

NOTES:

When learning something new, we all start out in a stage of UNCONSCIOUS INCOMPETENCE: we don't know what we don't know. A goal of PAIRS is to reach the stage of UNCONSCIOUS COMPETENCE, where the skills you learn become habits. Learning about relationship dynamics and the attitudes and skills that contribute to happy, lasting relationships will help you become aware that there may be things you're doing — or not doing — that are preventing you from experiencing the level of love, connection and fulfillment you most want. Developing new habits requires deciding what you want to change, changing it, and sustaining the change under stress. Patience is vital.

FINDING WHAT WE'RE LOOKING FOR

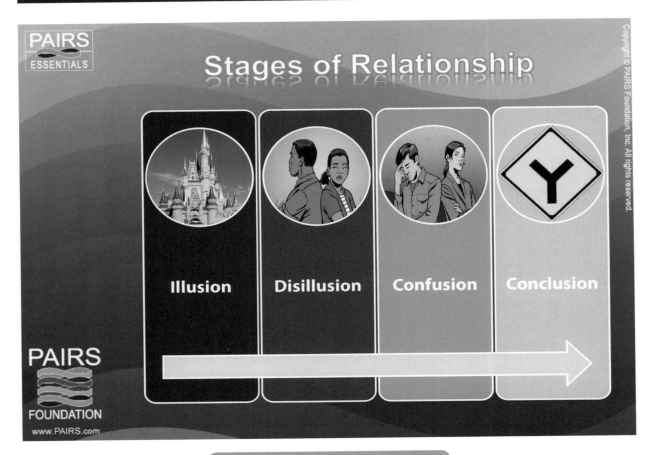

ILLUSION

Illusion - We are in love and hope that everything will be fine. We are looking for what is right in the other person and finding it. This stage can end as something happens that we didn't expect or something we did expect doesn't happen, leading to disappointment and ...

DISILLUSION

Disillusion - We begin to look for what is wrong, and we find that. Every human being has strengths, challenges and the potential for growth. It's easy to find what's wrong with another person when that's what we're looking for. That leads to the next stage, where we use whatever we know -- often including "dirty fighting" and "power struggles" -- to try to get what we want.

CONFUSION

Confusion - What is wrong, and how do I change it? Anger, pain, sadness and disappointment leak out in a variety of ways, such as blame, sarcasm, labeling, name calling, withholding, the silent treatment, etc. all of which lead to a ...

CONCLUSION

Conclusion - that often becomes despair, the end of intimacy, trust, confiding and joy. Or you open yourself to learn the skills to deal with conflict fairly and non-destructively and with goodwill -- so you don't need to lose each other and dreams that were once cherished.

THREE HOPES

1. *All the good things I ever wanted in my life, I will find with you.*

2. *All the good things I had, I will keep.*

3. *All the upsetting, unhappy things that happened to me before, will NOT happen with you.*

FIVE QUESTIONS FOR CLARIFYING EXPECTATIONS

What are you getting in your relationship that you do want?

_____

_____

_____

_____

_____

_____

What do you want from the relationship that you are not getting?

_____

_____

_____

_____

_____

_____

THREE FEARS

1 *Good things I hoped for will not or are not happening.*

2 *Good things I had, I will or I am losing.*

3 *Upsetting, hurtful things that happened before are happening again with you.*

What are you getting in the relationship that you don't want?

_____

_____

_____

_____

What are you giving in the relationship that you don't want to give?

_____

_____

_____

_____

What would you like to give to your partner if things were better between you?

_____

_____

_____

_____

PAIRS
ESSENTIALS

RELATIONSHIP ROAD MAP: PAIN OR PLEASURE

NOTES:

Biologically-Based Needs: Air, Food, Water, Shelter and Bonding. When needs are unmet, life is often experienced on the PAIN side of the Road Map, including feelings of dis-ease (which can turn to disease), distress, distrust, UNHAPPINESS, pain, danger (the anticipation of pain), fear and anger. Bonding (the unique combination of emotional openness and physical closeness with another person), is the only biologically-based need that we can't meet by ourselves. We need another person. Meeting each other's needs for bonding is an important aspect of the work of a relationship.

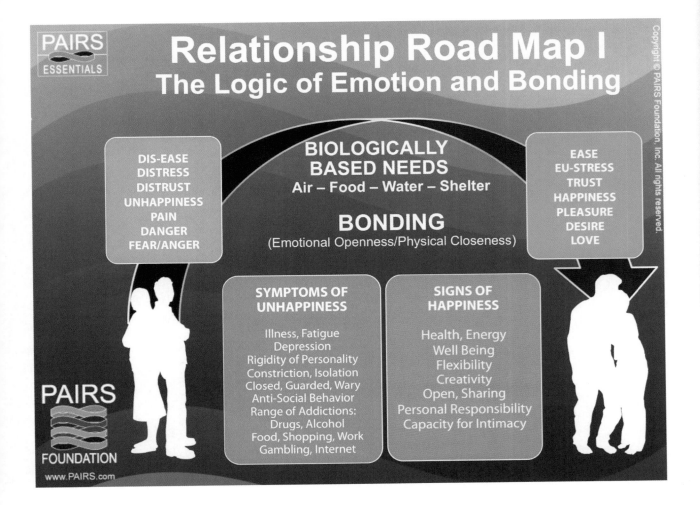

NOTES:

When our needs are met, we are more likely to experience life on the PLEASURE side of the Road Map, including feelings of ease, eu-stress (healthy stress, also known as the runner's high), trust, HAPPINESS, pleasure, desire, and love. Signs of Happiness include: health, energy, flexibility, creativity, sharing, personal responsibility, capacity for intimacy. Symptoms of Unhappiness include: illness, fatigue, depression, rigidity, constriction, isolation, closed, guarded, wary, anti-social behaviors, and the range of addictions. PAIRS is about skills to live life on the PLEASURE side.

STRESS STYLES OF COMMUNICATION

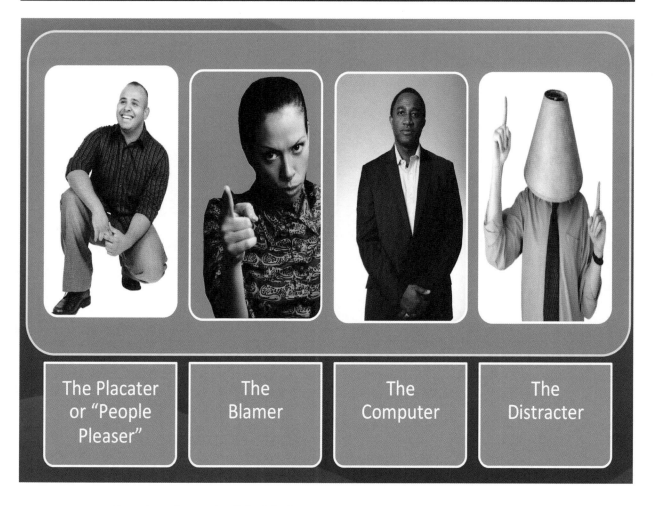

| The Placater or "People Pleaser" | The Blamer | The Computer | The Distracter |

Based on the work of Virginia Satir. Learn more in "New Peoplemaking."

NOTES:

Under stress, the PLACATER cancels out their own thoughts, feelings and needs, is eager to please, and has a hard time saying 'no.' Inside, the PLACATER can feel taken for granted and build up resentment towards others. Under stress, the BLAMER believes the best defense is a good offense. This communication style is one where the other person's needs and feelings are not taken into account. For the BLAMER, it is "all about me!" Inside, the BLAMER feels lonely because often no one wants to be around him/her. BLAMERS are often angry because they anticipate not getting what they want, including approval. Passively or actively, notice how the styles push others away.

INTERFERE WITH EMOTIONAL OPENNESS

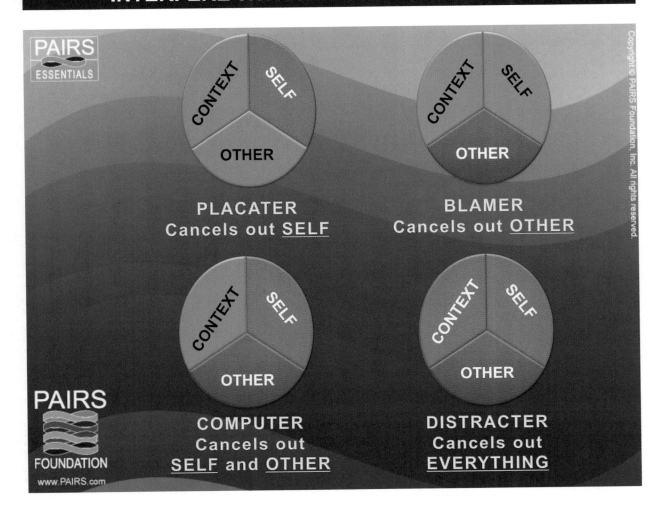

PLACATER
Cancels out <u>SELF</u>

BLAMER
Cancels out <u>OTHER</u>

COMPUTER
Cancels out
<u>SELF</u> and <u>OTHER</u>

DISTRACTER
Cancels out
<u>EVERYTHING</u>

PAIRS ESSENTIALS

PAIRS FOUNDATION
www.PAIRS.com

NOTES:

Under stress, the COMPUTER is the calm, cool and very reasonable one. The COMPUTER expresses no feelings and so it is difficult for them to get their needs met. The COMPUTER is careful to choose the right words and prefers to avoid mistakes. Inside, the COMPUTER decides, "I will not share my feelings and I don't know what to do with your feelings either." The DISTRACTER ignores everything....the feelings and the problem. With the DISTRACTER, you may notice avoidance of direct eye contact and direct answers, as well as changes to the subject being talked about. Inside, the DISTRACTER feels frightened, confused, distrustful, and believes: "I don't know what to do."

NOTES:

How often is your "style" of communication more of an issue than the issue itself? While each of us may have a primary style, we may have different styles in different relationships and situations. It's not uncommon to be in one style and then suddenly in another, depending on the issue or other person's reaction. When communicating in these stress styles, ask yourself: Do you feel heard? Do you feel understood? How do you feel towards yourself? How do you feel towards the other person? These styles create emotional distance instead of closeness and understanding, and can sabotage the ability to meet each other's needs for bonding. Learn more at apps.pairs.com/stress_styles.

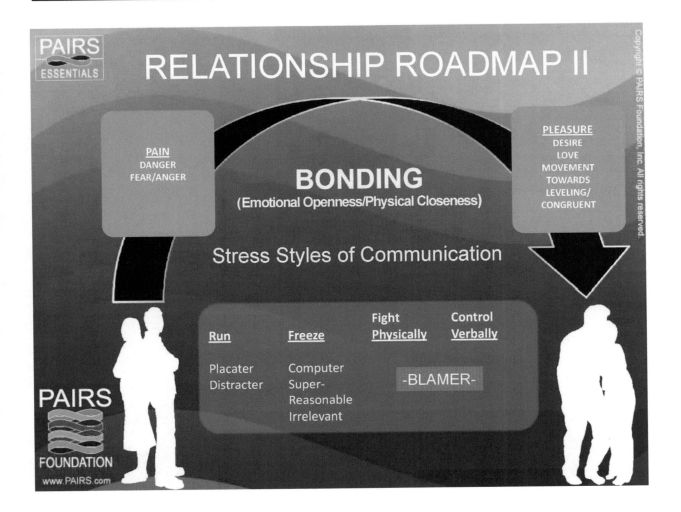

NOTES:

The PLACATER and DISTRACTER run away by cancelling out their own feelings and needs. The DISTRACTER, like the COMPUTER, can also be a way of freezing -- like a deer caught in the headlights, not knowing what to do with feelings so pretending they don't exist. BLAMERS fight, often needlessly escalating conflict and creating distance. All of these styles will keep us stuck on the PAIN side of the Relationship Road Map. The "Emotional Openness" aspect of Bonding means learning to level with each other with empathy, maturity, and a desire for the relationship to win. Each style also has some positive aspects. Can you identify them?

LEVELING STYLE PROMOTES EFFECTIVE COMMUNICATION

NOTES:

The LEVELER combines positive aspects of the stress styles. What's positive about the PLACATER style is empathy, as long as it's sincere and doesn't lead to acting one way when you're really feeling something else. The BLAMER's positive aspect is speaking on your own behalf, but with empathy and concern for the other person. The COMPUTER's positive trait is the ability to use knowledge and resources to find solutions, so long as you don't cancel out your own feelings in yourself or the other person. The DISTRACTER style can bring fun and pleasure into the relationship, as long as you return to address the issues later and don't develop a habit of avoiding opportunities for growth.

DTR FOR NURTURING RELATIONSHIPS

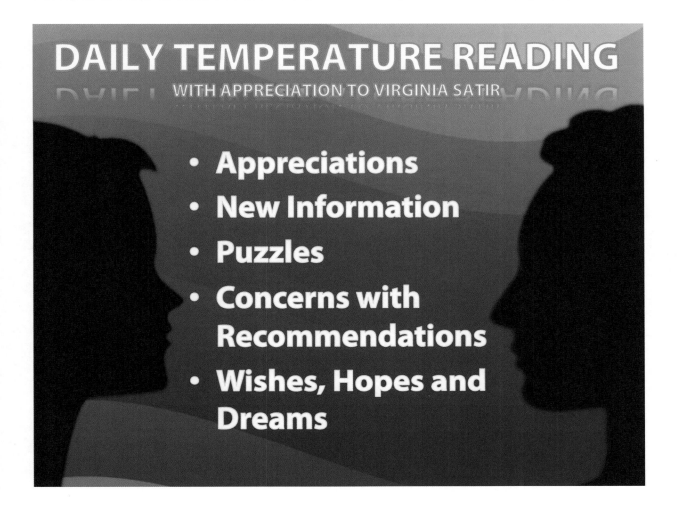

DAILY TEMPERATURE READING
WITH APPRECIATION TO VIRGINIA SATIR

- **Appreciations**
- **New Information**
- **Puzzles**
- **Concerns with Recommendations**
- **Wishes, Hopes and Dreams**

NOTES:

The DAILY TEMPERATURE READING, also known as the "DTR," is a tool for watering the garden of your most important relationships. With practice, the DTR becomes a habit, making it natural to look for — and express — appreciations to one another, keep each other up-to-date on the developments in our lives, ask questions about anything we're wondering about so we don't have to assume, express concerns directly along with specific recommendations for change, and talk about our individual and shared goals for the future. Many graduates have said using the DTR on a regular basis was the most important tool for intentionally creating and sustaining thriving relationships.

ESSENTIALS

GOOD TALKING AND GOOD LISTENING

GOOD TALKING: *Making Sure the Intended Message is Received*

Good talking is DIRECT. To send a message that other people can be sure to "catch," you need to say what you mean. Don't "talk around" the subject. Don't just drop hints or make other people guess. Get to the point!

Good talking is CLEAR. Make certain that people can understand what you're saying and don't just have a "snowy picture" of it. You need to describe things well. You need to make sure that you aren't confusing your listener!

Good talking is SPECIFIC. Sending a message well means giving your listener all the necessary information. Don't be vague or general when you talk. Include details that can help the other person know exactly what you're talking about.

Good talking is HONEST. For your message to do the most good, it needs to be honest. Don't say something you really don't think or feel, or that doesn't match the facts.

Good talking is TACTFUL. Being tactful means being kind. You have to think about others feelings and rights before you speak. You do want to be direct, clear, specific, and honest with them. But you don't want to say things - accidentally or on purpose - that will hurt them unnecessarily. Words can hurt.

GOOD LISTENING: *Listening to Understand*

Good listening is ACTIVE. Good listening is more than just waiting until you can talk or until the other person stops talking or truly says something that interests you. Good listening is doing your best to hear, understand, and help the person who is talking to fully express what they want you to know.

Good listening is ATTENTIVE. To listen well, you need to concentrate on what the other person is saying. Make sure you get the full message that they are sending. Don't try to guess what they mean. Don't try to do something else at the same time--like planning what you want to say next--you will probably miss something important!

Good listening is OPEN. Good listening means giving the other person the freedom to speak and giving you the freedom to learn something. To do this, you need an open mind--one that doesn't refuse to hear certain things. After the speaker finishes, you can decide whether you agree or you don't agree with what was said. But while the speaker is talking, you need to agree to fully listen.

Good listening is RESPECTFUL. Good listeners never interrupt a speaker in the middle of a sentence. They only start speaking after the other person finishes a sentence and pauses. This way, they make certain that they hear everything the other person wants to say, and that they don't make the other person feel worthless or angry.

Good listening is CAREFUL. To be a good listener, you need to ask the speaker right away about anything that you didn't hear well, that isn't clear, or that you didn't quite understand.

Learn more at apps.pairs.com/good_listening.

CONFIDING ABOUT A COMPLAINT OR CONCERN

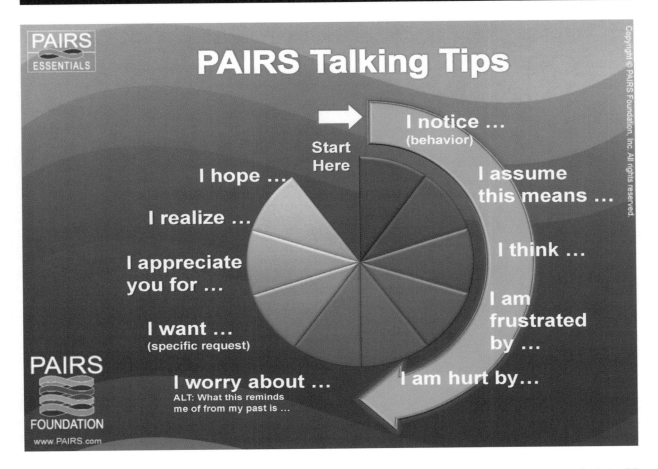

- Make sure you have enough time to give your undivided attention for a minimum of 10 to 15 minutes. Be fully present without distractions, with goodwill and empathy for each other.

- If you are the Speaker, use short sentences your partner can repeat back easily. Be aware of the intention behind your communication.

- As the Listener, repeat what you heard your partner say without exaggerating, adding comments, distorting or giving advice. Talking Tips is not a conversation; the Listener's role is to listen to understand and let the Speaker know that the message you are receiving is the message the Speaker intends. Listening to understand another person's perspective and feelings -- whether or not why see and feel the same way -- is a gift to the relationship.

- Use non-verbal cues such as nodding your head and making eye contact to show you are listening and that you understand. If facial expressions and body language communicate something different than the words, the words will not feel authentic.

- Validate the Speaker. The Listener's job is to help the speaker feel understood; not to agree, comment, judge, try to fix the problem, or get into a discussion.

- After completing Talking Tips, you can discuss the issue, reverse roles, or simply complete the exercise with appreciation for the information, awareness, perspective and understanding

- After first trying Talking Tips, you can practice online at apps.pairs.com/talkingtips or try an expanded version -- PAIRS Dialogue Guide -- at apps.pairs.com/dialogue_guide.

THE LOVE BANK

- Think of your relationship as a Love Bank. It's important to take time to build the balance of your account through regular deposits.

- We make deposits into our relationship Love Bank when we do things that leave our partner feeling cared about. Often what makes others feel cared about is different than what we want for ourselves.

- The Love Bank has a five-to-one rule: we must make at least five positive deposits in the Love Bank to neutralize one withdrawal, such as criticizing, making a negative observation, not keeping a promise or commitment, etc.

- Discovering what it takes to fill your relationship Love Bank with actions that say, "I care!" will help you grow closer in love, pleasure and connection. Make a commitment to keeping the balance high. A positive balance in the Love Bank helps provide important protection to our relationships.

NOTES:

The logic of love and emotions says we are naturally drawn to people who are a source of pleasure in our lives. That means different things to different people, and also changes over the course of a lifetime together. At one moment in our life, it may be connected to someone who helps us succeed in school or find a solution to a particular challenge; at another time, it could be about creating a home, raising children, achieving financial success, companionship, affection, having someone who brings new experiences to our lives, or anything in between. It's important to discover what's a pleasure to your partner and to recognize that many things change over time.

WHAT MAKES YOU FEEL CARED ABOUT?

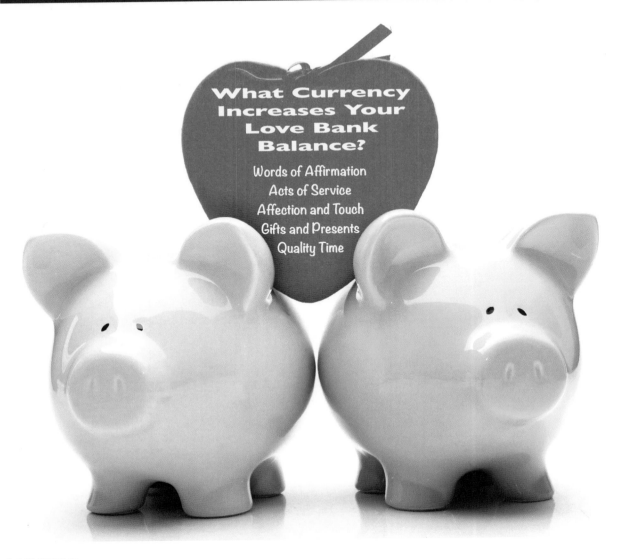

NOTES:

Don't assume that what makes you feel cared about is the same for your partner. As Dr. Gary Chapman writes in "The Five Love Languages," for some of us **WORDS OF AFFIRMATION** may be most important. For others it may be about **QUALITY TIME TOGETHER, AFFECTION AND TOUCH, GIFTS AND PRESENTS** or **ACTS OF SERVICE** that help accomplish goals, assignments, or chores. It's natural to have different ways of giving and receiving love in different relationships. Actions that say "I love you!" to a spouse may be very different than what makes a teenager feel cared about. **Learn more at apps.pairs.com/lovebank.**

CARING BEHAVIORS WORKSHEET

I feel cared about when …	How It Makes Me Feel	Enter check (√) marks when noticed
1.		
2.		
3.		
4.		
5.		
6.		
7.		
8.		
9.		
10.		
11.		
12.		

THIS PAGE MAY BE COPIED.

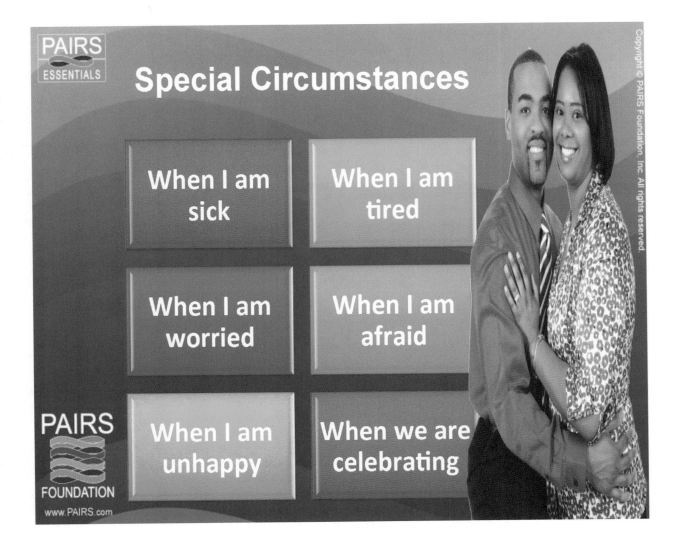

NOTES:

Lasting relationships involve navigating many of life's natural passages and transitions together. How do you and your loved ones experience and express love during periods of challenge, such as facing illness, fatigue, fear, sadness, and similar circumstances? What about in opposite situations, such as celebrating important milestones, accomplishments or successes? It's important to let others know what actions leave you feeling cared about in these situations, and also to know what makes others feel cared about when they are dealing with any of these special circumstances. Being able to safely confide in each other what you want in diffferent circumstances is vital.

ESSENTIALS

I'M BEGINNING TO REALIZE ...

_____

_____

_____

_____

_____

_____

_____

_____

_____

_____

_____

_____

_____

_____

VIRGINIA SATIR'S "FIVE FREEDOMS"

1. The Freedom to see and hear what is here instead of what should be, was, or will be.

2. The Freedom to say what one feels and thinks instead of what one should.

3. The Freedom to feel what one feels, instead of what one ought to.

4. The Freedom to ask for what one wants, instead of always waiting for permission.

5. The Freedom to take risks in one's own behalf, instead of choosing to be only 'secure' and not rocking the boat.

ESSENTIALS

PAIRS Satisfaction Survey

PAIRS cares about your personal experience. You may receive a brief survey or other follow-up from PAIRS Foundation by email asking about your experience. Add info@pairs.com to your email white list so we can reach you. Your response is important and appreciated!

Practice, Practice, Practice

PAIRS Essentials in an intensive introduction to powerful relationship building tools. Your classroom experience is just the first step. Practicing the skills until they become second nature will create new opportunities and resources that can be invaluable to happiness and success in your life.

Next Steps

1. Make time daily for Daily Temperature Readings. Make (and keep) a commitment of 15 to 20 minutes each day for Daily Temperature Readings for 30 days after you begin PAIRS. Remember to always use the DTR and other PAIRS tools with an invitation, goodwill and empathy.

2. Concerns with Recommendations are a natural part of all human relationships. You can share them inside the DTR by simply saying, "When _____ happens, I feel _____, and what I'd like instead is _____," or practice using Talking Tips to improve and deepen communication, understanding, and empathy.

3. Complete your Caring Behaviors Worksheets and make regular deposits in your relationship Love Bank!

4. Explore the exercises online at apps.pairs.com.

LEARNING POINTS:

- Levels of Learning
- Stages of Relationship
- Three Hopes/Three Fears
- Relationship Road Map
- Stress Styles of Communication
- **Leveling Style**
- **Daily Temperature Reading**
- **Talking Tips**
- **Love Bank**
- **Caring Behaviors**

Underlined topics are key tools in the PAIRS Essentials curriculum.

NOTES:

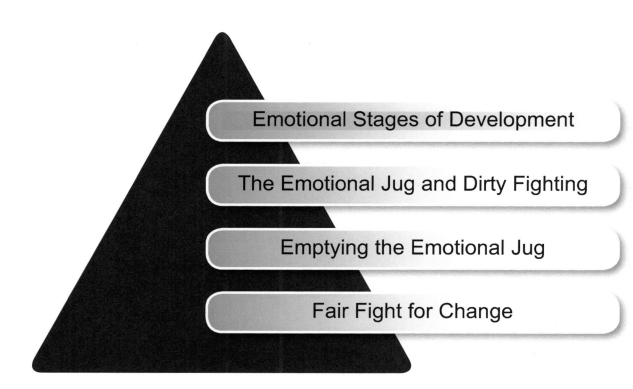

- Emotional Stages of Development
- The Emotional Jug and Dirty Fighting
- Emptying the Emotional Jug
- Fair Fight for Change

NOTES:

Conflict is a natural aspect of every close human relationship. More than the issues themselves, how loved ones deal with differences and disagreements is likely to determine the course of their relationship. No one chooses to share their life with another person to become enemies, yet trust and respect can be quickly sabotaged by active and passive dirty fighting tactics. Sustaining love requires learning to fight on the same side *for* the relationship when challenges arise. When couples are able to negotiate with goodwill, empathy and compassion, on the other side of most disagreements they discover deeper experiences of acceptance, understanding, respect, trust and feelings of love.

PAIRS FOUNDATION

CONSTRUCTIVE CONFLICT

Key goals

- Consider the impact of emotional attitudes on our ability to navigate differences and conflicts that naturally arise in close relationships.

- Discover the influence of painful, upsetting emotions on our ability to experience love and pleasure and understand how these feelings impact our behaviors.

- Learn the Emptying the Emotional Jug tool for safely confiding emotions on behalf of increased empathy and love.

- Practice the Fair Fight for Change tool for negotiating differences and conflicts on behalf of your relationship vision.

Topics and Tools

- Emotional Stages of Development
- The Emotional Jug
- Dirty Fighting
- Emptying the Emotional Jug
- Fair Fight for Change
- Time-Out Tip
- Fight Styles and Results Profile
- Guidelines for Coaches

PAIRS
ESSENTIALS

33

EMOTIONAL STAGES OF DEVELOPMENT

INFANT

"I want what I want when I want it!"

CHILD

Doesn't say what's wrong... acts it out in behavior and keeps you guessing.

ADOLESCENT

"Don't tell me what to do!"

ADULT

Capacity for mutual concern and empathy. Desire for the relationship to win.

The INFANT: Feels a need, but can only cry and must wait for the parents to figure out what the problem may be. <u>Adult 'stuck' in the EMOTIONAL INFANT</u>: Can treat others like an object to meet their needs. That person may be expressing: *"I want what I want when I want it, and you are just an object to give me what I want."*

The CHILD: Communicates, but remains dependent on others for meeting their needs; will act out feelings of hurt, fear and resentment. <u>Adult 'stuck' in the EMOTIONAL CHILD</u>: Will *act out* feelings of resentment through distance, pouting, whining, withholding, or placating. That person may say: *"You have things that I want and I will find a way to get them from you."* The Emotional Child is not honest and will not negotiate openly in the relationship.

The ADOLESCENT: Is rebellious with parents and authority figures and in effect says, "Don't tell me what to do!" Has a need to prove they are not dependent. <u>Adult 'stuck' in the EMOTIONAL ADOLESCENT</u>: Cannot give their partner what they want without feeling controlled by them and resenting it. That person may say: *"I cannot listen to you with empathy because I believe you are telling me what to do. You are being critical of me, my beliefs, and my behavior."* Whatever the partner asks for is experienced as control and feels as if they are being treated like a child.

The EMOTIONAL ADULT: Has the capacity to demonstrate goodwill and mutual concern, is open to learning, growing and has a willingness to change. The healthy Emotional Adult will say: *"I can ask for what I need and want, without controlling, manipulating or running from you; I can listen with empathy about how it is for you, without assuming it's only about me."*

One of the important tasks of a loving marriage is that each person functions as an EMOTIONAL ADULT, enough of the time, to resolve problems and is able to give each other support and caring.

DIRTY FIGHTING TACTICS: ACTIVE AND PASSIVE

DIRTY FIGHTING TACTICS	What I do.	What my Partner does.	What my Partner will say I do.
SARCASM			
RIDICULING			
THREATENING			
ACCUSING			
LABELING			
TAUNTING			
LAUGHING AT			
ASSUMING			
SNEERING			
CONTEMPT			
IGNORING			
BLAMING			
STONEWALLING			
CRITICIZING			
LYING			
OTHER			
OTHER			

PAIRS
ESSENTIALS

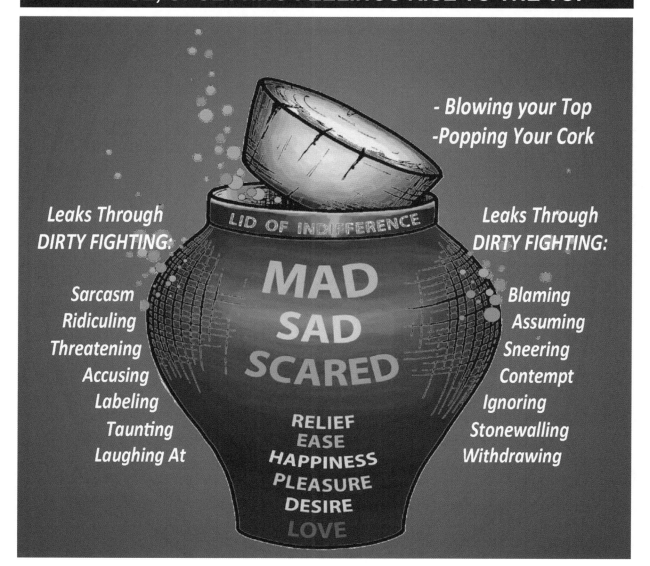

PAINFUL, UPSETTING FEELINGS RISE TO THE TOP

- Blowing your Top
- Popping Your Cork

LID OF INDIFFERENCE

MAD
SAD
SCARED

RELIEF
EASE
HAPPINESS
PLEASURE
DESIRE
LOVE

Leaks Through
DIRTY FIGHTING:

Sarcasm
Ridiculing
Threatening
Accusing
Labeling
Taunting
Laughing At

Leaks Through
DIRTY FIGHTING:

Blaming
Assuming
Sneering
Contempt
Ignoring
Stonewalling
Withdrawing

NOTES:

The EMOTIONAL JUG is a way to think about emotions/feelings. Imagine pouring all of your feelings into a big jug. The feelings would settle in different layers. At the very top may be a 'cork' that tries to keep upsetting emotions from leaking out. The feelings that rise to the top are the more intense emotions, such as anger, fear, and sadness. It's not easy to think clearly when painful feelings get jumbled up together, let alone to feel happiness, love, tenderness or desire. Guilt, jealousy, and shame are also feelings that can fill the jug. Painful feelings may eventually implode or explode. On the way, they often leak through dirty fighting. Learn more at apps.pairs.com/emotionaljug.

EMPTYING THE EMOTIONAL JUG

What are you **MAD** about?	• *If you were mad about anything else, what would it be? Thank You!*
What are you **SAD** about?	• *If you were sad about anything else, what would it be? Thank You!*
What are you **SCARED** about?	• *If you were scared about anything else, what would it be? Thank You!*
What are you **GLAD** about?	• *Is there anything else that you are glad about? Thank You!*

- Make sure you have enough time to give your undivided attention, which should be a minimum of 20 to 30 minutes. Listener must be fully present to the Speaker without distractions.

- When you're first learning, practice Emptying the Emotional Jug with issues that are not about the Listener. This is a confiding exercise, not a discussion.

- The Listener is fully present with empathy - not judgment, defensiveness, the need to "fix it," ask questions, disqualify, minimize feelings, or interject their own experiences.

- If you are the Speaker, simply express what's there at each step of the exercise. It's not necessary to get into a discussion; feelings are in your gut, not your head.

- The Listener should use non-verbal cues that show good listening and empathy.

- After completing Emptying the Jug, show appreciation to each other for sharing, listening, and making more room for uplifting feelings that make it posssible to experience greater connection, love and happiness.

FAIR FIGHT FOR CHANGE PROCESS IN TEN STEPS

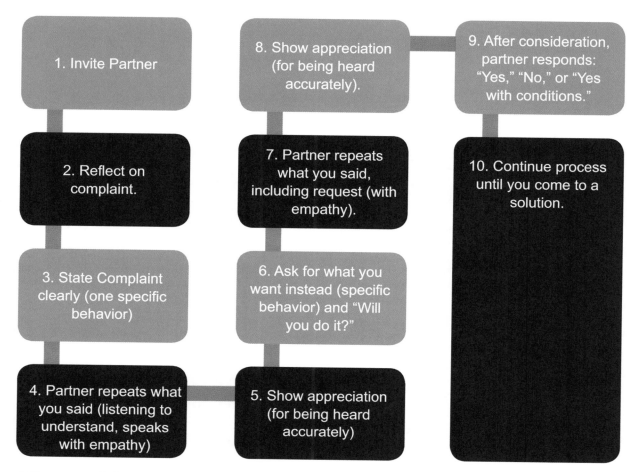

1. Invite Partner

2. Reflect on complaint.

3. State Complaint clearly (one specific behavior)

4. Partner repeats what you said (listening to understand, speaks with empathy)

5. Show appreciation (for being heard accurately)

6. Ask for what you want instead (specific behavior) and "Will you do it?"

7. Partner repeats what you said, including request (with empathy).

8. Show appreciation (for being heard accurately).

9. After consideration, partner responds: "Yes," "No," or "Yes with conditions."

10. Continue process until you come to a solution.

When practicing the Fair Fight for Change with coaches, think of the orange lines as the opportunity to share aloud the inner dialogue you have throughout the process.

NOTES:

The Fair Fight for Change is used to confide a complaint and request a change in behavior. It is a negotiation on behalf of the relationship, not against either person. Differences are a natural part of every close relationship. The fair fight process is to benefit you, your partner, and your relationship. Feeling that your partner really understands is very important. Often what lies behind a specific complaint is a request to feel heard and understood. Empathic listening is as important as sending the message. Coaching helps participants learn to stay on track, clearly focus on one specific issue (that's open to negotiation), voice their inner dialogue, and develop comfort with the process.

IF FEELING OVERWHELMED, CALL "TIME-OUT"

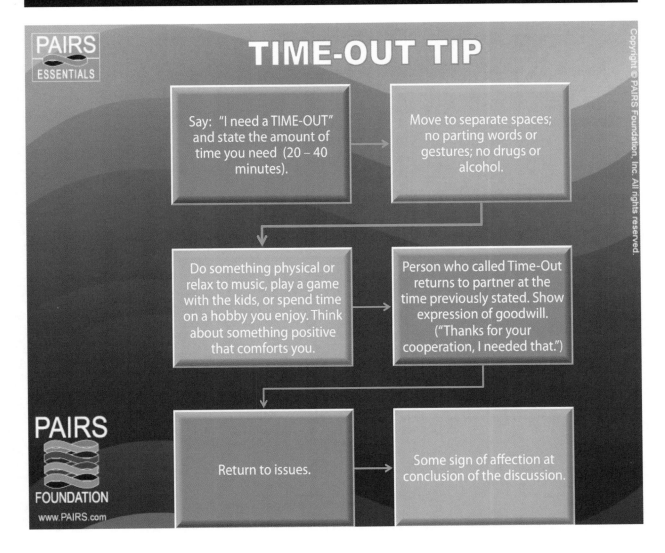

TIME-OUT TIP

Say: "I need a TIME-OUT" and state the amount of time you need (20 – 40 minutes).

Move to separate spaces; no parting words or gestures; no drugs or alcohol.

Do something physical or relax to music, play a game with the kids, or spend time on a hobby you enjoy. Think about something positive that comforts you.

Person who called Time-Out returns to partner at the time previously stated. Show expression of goodwill. ("Thanks for your cooperation, I needed that.")

Return to issues.

Some sign of affection at conclusion of the discussion.

www.PAIRS.com

NOTES:

Especially when dealing with differences, it's important to stay grounded with goodwill, empathy, openness to learning, and negotiating solutions that will help your relationship succeed. Often, the price someone pays for getting what they want may be to sabotage far more meaningful dreams. It's helpful to agree ahead of time that if you're in a Fair Fight for Change and you find yourself feeling overwhelmed, you can call Time-Out for 20-40 minutes to give yourself a chance to calm down, relax, and then return to each other in touch with what's most important to you, able to confide, listen with empathy, and find answers that work for your relationship.

FIGHT STYLE PROFILE

Style	Fair	Unfair
Facial Expression	Open, Responsive, Reflective, Interested, Real	Closed, Guarded, Impassive, Masked, Disinterested
Focus	Here and Now, Direct, Specific to the Problem, One Issue, To the Point	Past, Generalizing, Gunny sacking, Kitchen Sink
Communication	Clear & Relevant, Shared Meaning, Responsive, Accurate Feedback, Empathy	No Empathy, One Way, Inaccurate or No Feedback
Information & Reality	Realistic, Accurate, Authentic	Distorted, Exaggerated, Fantasy, Lies
Comments & Impact	Reasonable, Fair, Above the Belt	Not Open to Other Person's Perspective, Feelings and Experience
Responsibility	Willing to Recognize Own Contribution to the Problem	Justifying, Denying, Ignoring Own Role
Openness to Change	Willing and Open to Change	Rigid, Fixed, Unchanging

Adapted from "The Intimate Enemy: How to Fight Fair in Love and Marriage," by George Bach and Peter Wyden.

PAIRS FOUNDATION

FIGHT RESULTS PROFILE

Profile	Constructive	Destructive
Importance	Feel More Important to Partner	Feel Less Important to Partner
Influence & Self-Worth	Increased – Feel Heard and Understood	Decreased – Feel Misunderstood
Resentment	Relieved	Inhibited, Repressed
Hurt & Fear	Decreased	Increased
Trust	Increased	Decreased
Closeness	Feel Closer, More Affectionate	Feel More Distant
Reparation	Hurts Mended – Willing to or Did Make Up for Mistakes or Mistreatment	No Attempt to Make Up for Mistakes or Hurt Feelings
Forgiveness	Able to Forgive Partner	Desire to Withhold, Withdraw, Distance or Get Even
Progress	Progress Made Toward Solution	No Progress Made Toward Solution

HELPING COUPLES FIND THEIR OWN ANSWERS

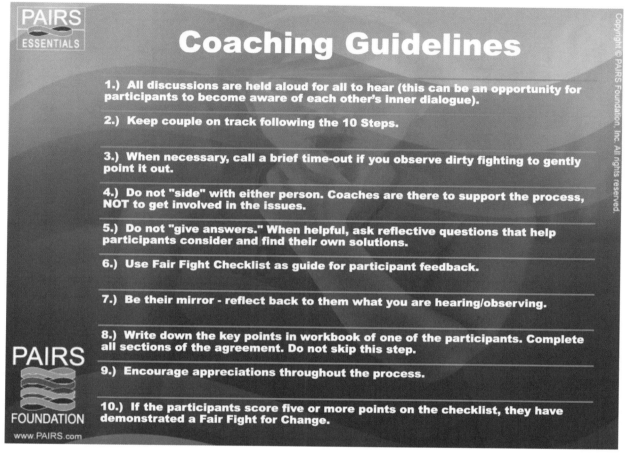

PAIRS ESSENTIALS

Coaching Guidelines

1.) All discussions are held aloud for all to hear (this can be an opportunity for participants to become aware of each other's inner dialogue).

2.) Keep couple on track following the 10 Steps.

3.) When necessary, call a brief time-out if you observe dirty fighting to gently point it out.

4.) Do not "side" with either person. Coaches are there to support the process, NOT to get involved in the issues.

5.) Do not "give answers." When helpful, ask reflective questions that help participants consider and find their own solutions.

6.) Use Fair Fight Checklist as guide for participant feedback.

7.) Be their mirror - reflect back to them what you are hearing/observing.

8.) Write down the key points in workbook of one of the participants. Complete all sections of the agreement. Do not skip this step.

9.) Encourage appreciations throughout the process.

10.) If the participants score five or more points on the checklist, they have demonstrated a Fair Fight for Change.

PAIRS FOUNDATION
www.PAIRS.com

Coaches often learn much that can help their relationships by guiding others through the Fair Fight for Change. No matter how tempting, don't get in the way of participants experiencing, and perhaps struggling, through the process of identifying and negotiating their own solutions.

NOTES:

As coaches, it can be tempting to offer advice or a solution during the Fair Fight for Change. Remember, the goal is for participants to learn to use the process to negotiate their own solutions. While coaches may have excellent ideas for resolving a particular issue or conflict, this process is about couples discovering they can find their own answers. Whatever the issue is today, there will be other issues in the future. The role of coaches is to help participants learn to stay in the safe structure of the Fair Fight for Change process, gently call attention to any dirty fighting (when necessary), and support the couple learning to fight for the relationship, not against each other.

FAIR FIGHT CHECKLIST (SCORECARD)

After the Fair Fight for Change is completed, place a check (√) in the box that best scores the participants in the fair fight. If one person gets a "No," place a check mark in the 'No' box. Add up the number of marks in each box for a total score. A score of five or more in the 'Yes' column indicates a successful Fair Fight for Change. If the total score is less than five, as time allows, the process should begin over.

Fair Fight Participants	YES	NO
Positive facial expressions and body language?		
Stayed on one complaint/concern?		
Communicated their feelings?		
Partner who was listening showed empathy?		
Participants shared appreciations?		
Came to a solution?		
Demonstrated goodwill?		
TOTAL SCORE		

ESSENTIALS

FAIR FIGHT FOR CHANGE
Relationship Agreement

Specific, Measurable Behaviors:
As distinct from attitude or character
changes, and wishful hopes or possibilities.

How this agreement will benefit our relationship:
Include both partner's perspectives.

Duration of this agreement:
You can always chose to extend the
agreement longer if it is working well.

Schedule times for review and tune-up:
Remember that breakdowns are
learning opportunities.

Our reminders for keeping this agreement alive:
Auditory or visual reminders that inspire
you to action.

ADDITIONAL NOTES:

_____

_____

_____

_____

_____

_____

THIS PAGE MAY BE COPIED.

RELATIONSHIP AGREEMENT

FAIR FIGHT FOR CHANGE
Relationship Agreement

Specific, Measurable Behaviors:
*As distinct from attitude or character
changes, and wishful hopes or possibilities.*

How this agreement will benefit our relationship:
Include both partner's perspectives.

Duration of this agreement:
*You can always chose to extend the
agreement longer if it is working well.*

Schedule times for review and tune-up:
*Remember that breakdowns are
learning opportunities.*

Our reminders for keeping this agreement alive:
*Auditory or visual reminders that inspire
you to action.*

ADDITIONAL NOTES:

_____

_____

_____

_____

_____

_____

_____

THIS PAGE MAY BE COPIED.

I'M BEGINNING TO REALIZE ...

_____
_____
_____
_____
_____
_____
_____
_____
_____
_____
_____
_____
_____
_____
_____
_____
_____
_____
_____
_____
_____
_____
_____

PAIRS FOUNDATION

ESSENTIALS

Watch Your Email for PAIRS Follow-Up

You may receive additional information about the materials in this session of PAIRS Essentials directly from PAIRS Foundation. Please be sure info@pairs.com is on your email white list so you don't miss follow-up information from PAIRS.

Practice, Practice, Practice

PAIRS Essentials in an intensive introduction to powerful relationship building tools. Your classroom experience is just the first step. Practicing the skills until they become second nature will create new opportunities and resources that can be invaluable to happiness and success in your life.

Next Steps

1. Continue to make time for Daily Temperature Readings.

2. Look for an opportunity to invite your significant other to Empty the Emotional Jug; practice being fully present with empathy and goodwill. Ask your partner to be present for you to practice too. If you have age-appropriate children at home, consider teaching the exercise to them. Children should be the speakers.

3. Be aware of instances in which dirty fighting takes place. If you find yourself dirty fighting, pause to reflect on what you've discovered in PAIRS and ways to deal with differences using the skills you're learning.

4. Support each other in honoring your Fair Fight for Change Relationship Agreement.

5. Explore PAIRS toolkit online at www.pairs.com/toolkits.

LEARNING POINTS:

- Emotional Stages of Development

- Emotional Jug

- Dirty Fighting

- **Emptying the Emotional Jug**

- **Fair Fight for Change**

- Fight Style Profile

- Fight Results Profile

- Fair Fight Checklist

* *Underlined topics are key tools in the PAIRS Essentials curriculum.*

NOTES:

_____

_____

_____

_____

_____

_____

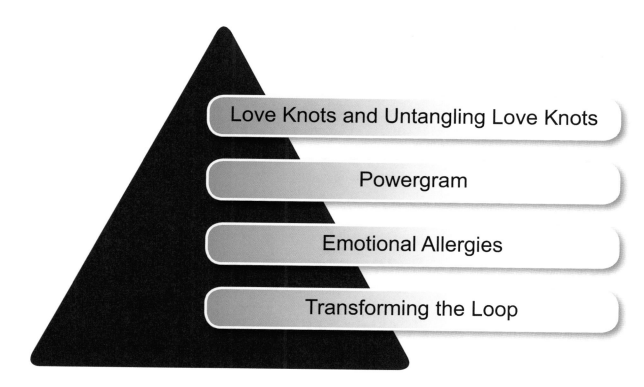

Love Knots and Untangling Love Knots

Powergram

Emotional Allergies

Transforming the Loop

NOTES:

_____

_____

_____

_____

_____

_____

_____

EMOTIONAL LITERACY

Key goals

- Uncover and reconsider Love Knots, the hidden expectations and assumptions that are unique to intimate relationships.

- Create a model for shared decision-making and accountability based on your personal relationship vision and mutual respect.

- Identify causes of intense emotional reactions and consider the impact on close relationships.

- Learn a process for transforming reactions and patterns that can lead to distance and relationship distress into increased empathy, understanding and love.

Topics and Tools

- **Love Knots**

- **Untangling Love Knots**

- **Powergram**

- **Emotional Allergies**

- **Emotional Allergy Infinity Loop**

- **Transforming the Loop**

HIDDEN ASSUMPTIONS AND EXPECTATIONS

Hidden assumptions and expectations can create distance and misunderstanding in relationships.

Love Knots are commonly held beliefs that seem to be true. However, they are not true because they are not based on logical, realistic thinking. Love Knots can be very harmful to a relationship.

PAIRS Founder Lori Gordon identified dozens of hidden assumptions and expectations many couples have about their relationships.

Consider these examples to see which may be interfering with intimacy in your life. You can also learn more at apps.pairs.com/loveknots.

Love Knot # 1

"If you really loved me, you would know what I want, and you would do it. Since you don't, you obviously don't care."

Untangled

"I cannot assume that you know what I want and need. I will ask for what I want and not expect you to know."

Reflection

When have you waited for others to guess what you want and do it, becoming disappointed, hurt, or distant when they didn't?

What happened as a result?

_____

_____

TYPICAL LOVE KNOTS

Love Knot # 2

"When I tell you how I feel, you interrupt, disagree, give advice, judge, or dismiss my feelings. I stop telling you. I distance myself from you."

Untangled

"If I want you to listen to me and to hear me without comment, I need to ask for that. Advice is not helpful when the person does not want it. Learning how to listen more attentively is often more important than giving advice."

Reflection

Are there people in your life who you've stopped confiding in because you didn't like their reaction? How has that affected your relationships?

What might be possible in your relationship if you could ask your partner to just listen with empathy?

_____

_____

Love Knot # 3

"If you are in pain, I believe I should be able to fix it. I don't know how to fix it, so I feel inadequate. I get angry with you for making me feel inadequate. I withdraw from you and blame you when you are in pain."

Untangled

"When you are in pain I can be supportive without believing I have to provide a solution. I can listen, empathize and acknowledge what you say. I will respect and honor your feelings as well as your ability to ask for what you want."

Reflection

Have there been times in your life when you couldn't make things better for someone you cared about? How did you feel about the situation? About yourself? About the other person?

How can you be supportive of someone going through a difficult time? What would you like from your partner when you are in pain?

_____

_____

ESSENTIALS

TYPICAL LOVE KNOTS

Love Knot # 4

"If I tell you what I want and you do it, it doesn't count (because I had to tell you). If you try to guess what I want and you don't get it right, I get angry."

Untangled

"I cannot expect you to know what I want. Nor can I expect you to do anything exactly the way I would. I can still appreciate the gift of whatever you do because you believe I would like it."

Reflection

How often have you experienced double binds in your relationships where no matter what happens, everyone loses? What happens to love in these situations?

Reflect on a time you got angry because someone didn't do something the way you wanted. Can you also remember being on the receiving end of this double bind? What would help you appreciate others for what they do, even when it's not done exactly the way you want?

_____

Love Knot # 5

"If I let myself get close to you, I will need you. If I am too dependent and need (love) too much, I will not be able to survive without you. I will become weak."

Untangled

"I can enjoy being close to you, yet survive on my own if I need to. As an adult I am not helpless. I can make a new life for myself if I have to. Meanwhile, the pleasures of intimacy are among life's most fulfilling gifts."

Reflection

This can be a self-fulfilling prophecy. Can you remember a situation where your fear of losing someone or something important to you led to exactly what you most feared? Sometimes fears about the future can be so powerful that we miss opportunities to experience love, happiness, pleasure and fulfillment in the present.

What fears about the future are getting in the way of embracing the gift of closeness and connection with those who are most important in your life today?

_____

TYPICAL LOVE KNOTS

Love Knot # 6

"If we don't agree, one of us must be wrong. If it's me, that means I am bad, stupid, ignorant, or inadequate. So it can't be me. I must prove that it's you so I won't feel like a failure."

Untangled

"We should be able to disagree. We are all unique, and disagreements are a natural reflection of our uniqueness."

Reflection

How do you feel when a significant other disagrees with you? What price has your relationship paid for arguments about different views and perspectives?

Consider a time when you argued or distanced from someone who was important in your life because you didn't agree. What would help you embrace future differences as a natural part of all relationships and become open to hearing and considering other views without having to agree with each other?

_____

Love Knot # 7

"If I ask what you are thinking or feeling, I believe I am intruding (as you would tell me if you wanted me to know). If I don't ask, you believe I'm not interested, so you never tell me. We live as strangers."

Untangled

"Confiding is the life blood of intimacy. I need to be able to ask for information, and you need to be able to volunteer it when I don't ask. If we are to nurture our relationship, it is crucial that we speak our truths, ask our questions, and keep each other informed."

Reflection

Remember a period in your life when it was natural to have open, flowing conversations together. How did that feel? What did it mean to you to know that you could talk about anything and everything with each other?

What does it mean to have a witness to your life, and to be a witness to someone else's life? What would make it natural and safe for others to share their thoughts and feelings with you? What do you need from others?

_____

YOUR LOVE KNOTS

Place a check (√) mark if a given Love Knot fits for you. Then place a question mark (?) in the next box if you suspect that Love Knot fits for your partner.

Love Knot #	Love Knot Description (May Reword to Fit)	Fits for me	Suspect Fits for my Partner
1.	If you really loved me, you would know what I want, and you would do it. Since you don't, you obviously don't care.		
2.	When I tell you how I feel, you interrupt, disagree, give advice, judge, or dismiss my feelings. That's not what I want. I stop telling you. I distance myself from you.		
3.	If you are in pain, I believe I should be able to fix it. I don't know how to fix it, so I feel inadequate. I get angry with you for making me feel inadequate. I withdraw from you and blame you for being in pain.		
4.	If I tell you what I want and you do it, it doesn't count (because I had to tell you). If you try to guess what I want and you don't get it right, I get angry.		
5.	If I let myself get close to you, I will need you. If I am too dependent and need (love) you too much, I will not be able to survive without you. I will become weak.		
6.	If we don't agree, one of us must be wrong. If it's me, that means I am bad, stupid, ignorant, or inadequate. So it can't be me. I must prove that it's you so I won't feel like a failure.		
7.	If I ask what you are thinking or feeling, I believe I am intruding (as you would tell me if you wanted me to know). If I don't ask, you believe I'm not interested, so you never tell me. We live as strangers.		

UNTANGLING A LOVE KNOT

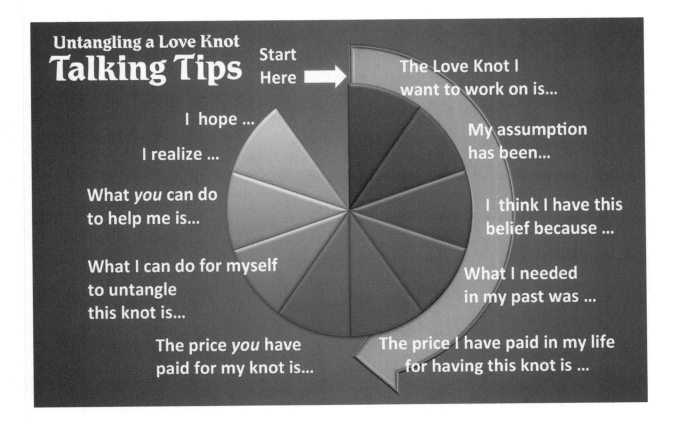

Untangling a Love Knot
Talking Tips

Start Here →

The Love Knot I want to work on is...

My assumption has been...

I think I have this belief because ...

What I needed in my past was ...

The price I have paid in my life for having this knot is ...

The price *you* have paid for my knot is...

What I can do for myself to untangle this knot is...

What *you* can do to help me is...

I realize ...

I hope ...

Learn more at apps.pairs.com/loveknots.

NOTES:

Be fully present without distractions, with goodwill and empathy for each other. If you are the Speaker, use short sentences your partner can repeat back easily. As the Listener, repeat what you think you heard your partner say without exaggerating, adding comments, distorting or giving advice. This is not a conversation. Use non-verbal cues that are encouraging to the speaker. Validate partner's thoughts and feelings. Help partner feel understood; do not agree, comment, judge, try to fix the problem, or get into a discussion. Afterwards, discuss the issue, reverse roles, or simply complete the exercise with appreciation for the information, awareness, perspective and understanding shared.

POWERGRAM - WHO DECIDES?

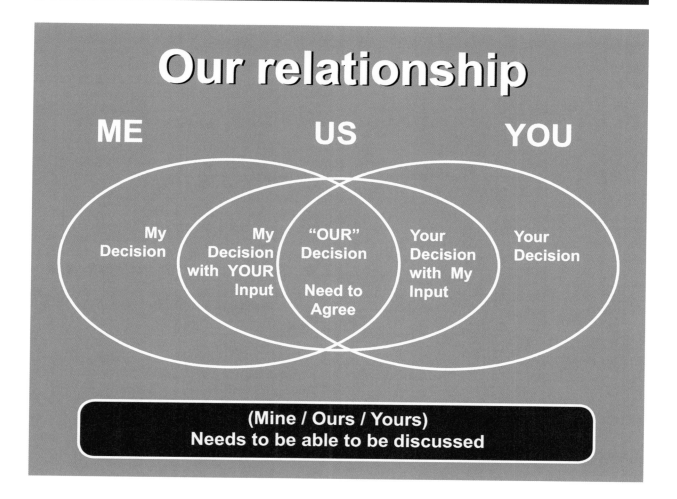

Our relationship

ME   US   YOU

My Decision

My Decision with YOUR Input

"OUR" Decision

Need to Agree

Your Decision with My Input

Your Decision

(Mine / Ours / Yours)
Needs to be able to be discussed

NOTES:

The Powergram is a helpful tool for heading off power struggles before they begin. Creating your Powergram together is a valuable opportunity to consider what's most important to you and your partner, the roles each of you will play in the relationship, and identify areas that require agreement. Your Powergram should reflect the unique values, vision and circumstances of your relationship. Be sure to re-visit your Powergram regularly. It's especially important to consider how your Powergram changes during special circumstances and as your life and family evolve.

PAIRS FOUNDATION

DECISION-MAKING WORKSHEET

Sample Decision Making Topic	My Decision	My Decision with Your Input	OUR Decision We Need To Agree	Your Decision with My Input	Your Decision
My Work Hours					
Cleaning Clothes					
Time to go to Bed					
Time Spent Together					
School Work					
Grocery Shopping					
Rules for the Children					
Changing Diapers					
Family Meals					
Lovemaking					
Household Budget					
Home Repairs					
Time Spent Apart					
Phone Calls					
Affection in Public/Private					
Relationships with Friends					
Taking a Vacation					
Retirement Plans					
Health/Life Insurance					
Other:					

PAIRS
ESSENTIALS

EMOTIONAL ALLERGY NEGATIVE INFINITY LOOP

My Allergy

My Feelings

My Belief

My Behavior

Your Allergy

Your Feelings

Your Belief

Your Behavior

Dirty Fighting　　**Dirty Fighting**

NOTES:

Having the intensity of an Emotional Allergy makes something feel much worse than the actual current situation might be. When we have an Emotional Allergy, we feel much worse than others might feel, and we wind up reacting with more intensity than others might understand or accept. It's as if we hand the bill for something someone did to us in the past to someone in the present. We can find ourselves stuck in an Emotional Allergy Negative Infinity Loop when our intense response triggers an Emotional Allergy in the other person.

EMOTIONAL ALLERGY NEGATIVE INFINITY LOOP

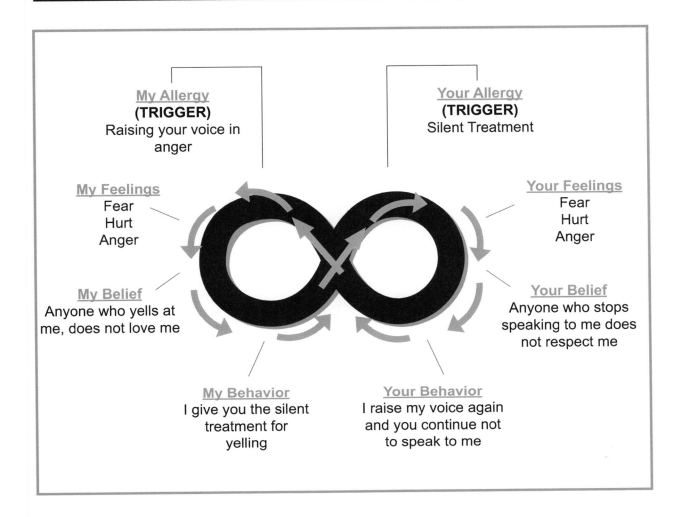

My Allergy
(TRIGGER)
Raising your voice in anger

Your Allergy
(TRIGGER)
Silent Treatment

My Feelings
Fear
Hurt
Anger

Your Feelings
Fear
Hurt
Anger

My Belief
Anyone who yells at me, does not love me

Your Belief
Anyone who stops speaking to me does not respect me

My Behavior
I give you the silent treatment for yelling

Your Behavior
I raise my voice again and you continue not to speak to me

NOTES:

The loop represents two separate people; each on their own side, yet joined and bonded to each other. Each brings their own unique emotional allergies. One person's loop can begin with a triggering event by the other person's behavior, as shown in the example above. Many couples spend years in cycles that lead to distance, disappointment, and the surrender of once cherished wishes, hopes and dreams. Learning to transform this Negative Infinity Loop into one that makes it possible to be healing to each other is a central goal of PAIRS Essentials.

IDENTIFYING EMOTIONAL ALLERGIES

An Emotional Allergy I have for myself is:

When my partner behaves by….

I feel…

I think…

I worry about….

I behave by…..

An Emotional Allergy I suspect I trigger in my partner is:

When I behave by…

My partner feels…

My partner remembers…

My partner believes…

My partner behaves by…

CONFIDING AN EMOTIONAL ALLERGY

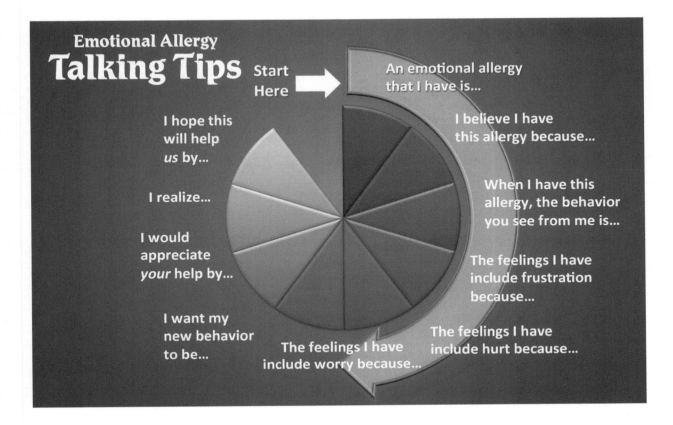

Learn more at apps.pairs.com/emotional_allergies.

NOTES:

As with the other Talking Tips exercises, be fully present without distractions, with goodwill and empathy for each other. As the Speaker, remember the importance of short sentences. As the Listener, remember to repeat back what you hear with empathy, without commenting, judging or getting into a conversation. Afterwards, you can discuss what you shared further, reverse roles, or simply complete the exercise with appreciation for the information, awareness, perspective and understanding shared.

ESSENTIALS

Partner One

My Allergy:
(TRIGGER)

To your raising your voice in anger

Confiding My Feelings of
Fear, Hurt, Anger

My Changed Belief:
You are not the person in my past.

You do love me. I can trust you to listen to my feelings and care.

My New Behavior (Confiding):

[You respond by listening with Empathy]

I Say: *When you yell at me, it scares me. I am afraid you will leave me like my father did.*

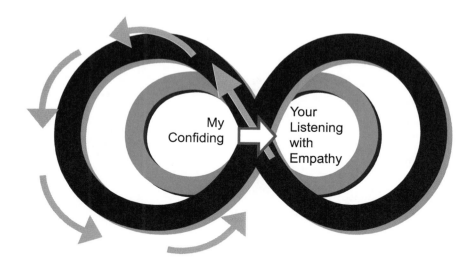

Partner Two

Your Changed Feelings
Sympathy

Your Changed Belief:
Its not against me.

Your Changed Behavior
Empathy, reassurance, affection, comfort

NOTES:

_____

_____

_____

_____

_____

_____

PAIRS FOUNDATION

LOOP OF VULNERABILITY AND EMPATHY

Vulnerability:

- *Allowing another person to see the parts of you that are scared, hurt, sad, and lonely, etc.*

- *Taking a risk to share your deepest thoughts and feelings with another person even when you are not sure how they will react.*

Empathy:

- *Imagining what it feels like to be in the other person's shoes.*

- *Imagining what that person thinks and feels.*

LOVE

NOTES:

When you become aware of intense feelings, you can choose to become reactive or to be vulnerable -- to allow another person to see the parts of you that are hurt, sad, afraid or angry. If the other person responds with empathy, you can create a positive Loop of Vulnerability and Empathy, which is easy to remember by the acronym: LOVE. Much of emotional intelligence (and success and happiness in life) is about the ability to pause when experiencing intense feelings, reflect on the possible source, and responding in ways that create closeness instead of distance.

ESSENTIALS

I'M BEGINNING TO REALIZE ...

_____
_____
_____
_____
_____
_____
_____
_____
_____
_____
_____
_____
_____
_____
_____
_____
_____
_____

> *"It is only with the heart that one can see clearly. What is essential is invisible to the eye."*
>
> *~Antoine de Saint-Exupéry*
> *The Little Prince*

64

ESSENTIALS

Watch Your Email for PAIRS Follow-Up

You may receive additional information about the materials in this session of PAIRS Essentials directly from PAIRS Foundation. Please be sure info@pairs.com is on your email white list so you don't miss follow-up information from PAIRS.

Practice, Practice, Practice

PAIRS Essentials in an intensive introduction to powerful relationship building tools. Your classroom experience is just the first step. Practicing the skills until they become second nature will create new opportunities and resources that can be invaluable to happiness and success in your life.

Next Steps

1. Continue to make time for Daily Temperature Readings.

2. Complete your Powergram and schedule a time for periodic review (monthly, quarterly, semi-annually).

3. Review the PAIRS Tool Kit and look for regular opportunities to continue practicing PAIRS skills.

4. Become more familiar with the online version of the PAIRS Tool Kit at www.pairs.com/toolkits. Make a habit of reviewing the tools there regularly.

5. Choose one ore more of the online exercises at apps.pairs.com that were not included in this class to reinforce and deepen your PAIRS training.

LEARNING POINTS:

- Love Knots

- **Untangling Love Knots**

- **Powergram**

- **Emotional Allergies**

- **Transforming the Loop**

* *Underlined topics are key tools in the PAIRS Essentials curriculum.*

NOTES:

_____

_____

_____

_____

_____

_____

ESSENTIALS

PAIRS ESSENTIALS TOOL KIT

Problem or feeling	Skill to use	To do for yourself	To do with your partner	Notes
Feeling disconnected	LEVELING STYLE	Take time to be fully present to the treasure that is you.	Get away from distractions to focus and be fully present to each other.	Create regular opportunities to connect with empathy and honesty.
Sense of growing distance	DAILY TEMPERATURE READING	Speak up for the relationship.	DTR will help strengthen intimacy and develop the habit of confiding.	Set aside time daily. Give hugs and be generous with appreciations.
Attempting to resolve problems under stress	TIME-OUT	Stop all talking immediately. State how much time you would like (20-40 minutes).	Do not continue to think badly of partner. Do not use drugs/ alcohol.	Resume talking to discuss and resolve the problems.
Wanting to feel cared about and loved	CARING BEHAVIORS LOVE BANK	Take care of you!	Add to Caring Behaviors list. Do several each day.	Revisit ways of filling your Love Bank.
Upsetting reaction to partner's behavior	TALKING TIPS	Review Talking Tips for yourself first.	Partner listens with empathy for understanding about what is troubling.	Listening partner repeats back until meaning is clear. No arguing.

PAIRS FOUNDATION

PAIRS ESSENTIALS TOOL KIT

Problem or feeling	Skill to use	To do for yourself	To do with your partner	Notes
Feeling emotionally overwhelmed	EMPTY THE JUG	Seek comfort and understanding.	Partner listens with empathy for understanding.	Thank your partner for having goodwill to listen to what you had to say. Show appreciation.
To ask for a behavior change from partner	FAIR FIGHT FOR CHANGE	Know what behavior change you want and why.	Invite partner for a FFFC and prepare to negotiate outcome.	Use Talking Tips or Time-Out to manage strong emotions. Stay to one subject.
Who should decide	POWERGRAM	Think through who should make the decision.	Use tools to discuss.	Need all tools: Good Talking, Good Listening, Talking Tips, Fair Fight for Change.
Full of resentment for partner	LOVE KNOTS	Identify your underlying belief.	Clarify with partner.	Reflect on what is true for partner rather than my assumptions.
Angry at partner's behavior	EMOTIONAL ALLERGY	Reflect on why you're so upset.	Use Talking Tips to explore your Emotional Allergy.	New understanding of feelings and reactions.

ESSENTIALS

NOTES AND REFLECTIONS

PAIRS
FOUNDATION

Made in the USA
Charleston, SC
21 May 2015